W9-ARV-282

THE SOLDIER THROUGH THE AGES
THE VIKING WARRIOR

Martin Windrow

Illustrated by
Angus McBride

Franklin Watts
London   New York   Toronto   Sydney

First published in Great Britain in 1984 by
Franklin Watts Ltd
12a Golden Square
London W1

First published in the USA by
Franklin Watts Inc.
387 Park Avenue South
New York
N.Y. 10016

First published in Australia by
Franklin Watts Australia
1 Campbell Street
Artarmon
NSW 2064

UK edition ISBN: 0 86313 179 4
US edition ISBN: 0-531-03816-5
Library of Congress Catalog Card
No: 84-51542

Designed by James Marks

Printed in Belgium

Contents

The sea wolves

In AD 793 the peaceful monastery on Lindisfarne, an island off the northeast coast of England, was sacked by merciless pagan pirates. Over the next 250 years a people who had previously been almost unknown to the rest of Europe became famous, and feared, all over the Western world. These were the Vikings – the fierce sea raiders from Scandinavia.

In their day they were known simply as the Norsemen – men from the north. The name Viking may come from their word for overseas voyaging. The greatest seamen of their times, they were also among the fiercest fighters. So bloodthirsty was their reputation that we tend to forget their other qualities. Legend paints them simply as cruel killers and robbers, which they were. But they were also great traders and merchant-explorers who made incredible voyages as far as the Caspian Sea in the east and Newfoundland in the west. And eventually they settled in many lands and became peaceful immigrants.

But to the terrified peoples of ninth-century Europe the Viking came as a

▷A Norse war chief prepares to sail on a trading and raiding voyage. His men load supplies and depart from their families. Some are landless warriors, supported by the chief's gifts from the plunder or profit they take by war or trade. Some are poor farmers, hoping to improve their fortunes.

Europe broke up into small, weak local kingdoms after the fall of the western Roman Empire in about AD 410. These had no armies of paid soldiers, full-time fighting men like Rome's legions. Life depended on farming, fishing and trading. The local leader kept a small bodyguard of chosen warriors, and all able-bodied men took up arms in times of war. Since they had no organization or supply system, they fought only in summer, living off the land as best they could.

punishment from God. The Vikings' own poems or sagas recall this as "a sword age . . . a wolf age;" and it is as sea wolves of the storm that we remember them, above all.

In Norway, Sweden and Denmark good farmlands, and therefore settlements, were thinly scattered. Norsemen lived in small, almost independent communities. They had no real "governments," and "kings" were simply local warrior chieftains. The only towns were trading posts.

Norway

Sweden

Denmark

The hungry land

The reasons why these fearless blond axe-men began to burst out of their cold northern lairs at the end of the eighth century are not completely understood. Their main motive for sailing the seas was probably the search for new homelands.

Most of Scandinavia was barren and mountainous, gripped by snow and ice for many months each year. The small areas of land fertile enough to grow crops could support only a small population. At the beginning of the Viking age there seems to have been a growth in the size of the population; so the Norsemen had to look overseas for new territories.

It seems that at about this time, too, the Scandinavians perfected their skills of ship-building and navigation. Now they had both a reason, and the means, to explore further afield. At first they probed the coasts of other lands and sailed up the great rivers, trading or raiding as chances offered. Where they found good land poorly defended, they returned with their families to settle permanently.

This caused long and bitter wars between

▷A Norse farmer watches longships sailing off on a raiding voyage in early summer. The eldest sons inherited the isolated, self-sufficient farms; so the younger, landless men sought their fortune overseas. The ships' captains planned voyages, then called for men to crew and fight for them in return for a share of the booty. Captains with a name for skill and good luck easily filled their ships.

the newcomers and the original inhabitants. Later, with the passing of time and with marriages between these peoples, the differences faded. In England, Ireland and northern France, where they had first come as raiders, the Norse settlers gradually merged into the local populations. Later generations inherited some of their strength and energy. For instance, the mighty Normans of northern France were simply descendants of Vikings who settled there under a famous leader named Hrolf the Ganger.

The longship

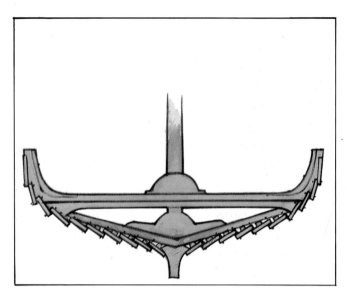

The ships in which the Vikings set sail were called "dragon ships," after the beast-head carvings sometimes seen on the stem-post. These boats were wonderfully seaworthy. Modern shipbuilders copied one discovered at Gokstad in Norway. It was found to sail at up to 11 knots, and would float in only 3 ft (1 m) of water, covering more than 220 miles (352 km) in a day. It was 76 ft (23.1 m) long, 17 ft (5.1 m) wide, and $6\frac{1}{2}$ ft (1.9 m) deep from keel to gunwale. This gave the boat a broad, shallow shape (*left*).

Longships had a single mast with a yard-arm and square sail. The mast could be lowered when the wind was unfavorable, or when going into a sea battle. The Gokstad ship had 16 oars on a side. It was made of oak planks, each cut from naturally curved timber, so the grain of the wood ran with the curve of the ship's sides. Supplies of dried and salted food, water bags, weapons and trade goods were stowed under a removable pine-plank deck. There were no rowing benches: it seems that Vikings sat on their sea chests to row. The Gokstad ship would have had a crew of about 70.

Steering was by a side-mounted rudder or steering oar fixed to the stern with ropes. The modern copy of this rough-looking arrangement was found to be very efficient and easy for a helmsman to control even in rough water. The Gokstad ship, fully laden, weighed about 18 tons.

Vikings sometimes hung their shields along the ships' sides for display when sailing home up sheltered fjords. This was also done to stop arrows in sea battles, but probably only in calm seas.

◁A ship nears completion in a Norse boatyard. The planks ready to be riveted are held in place by wooden peg-like clamps. Planks below the waterline, although riveted together, were only tied to the ribs with spruce roots, so the ship "worked" in heavy seas, moving with the rhythm of the waves. This flexible hull, with its deep, heavy keel, was stable and seaworthy.

The Viking's war gear

The Viking was not a soldier in the modern sense. He spent as much time being a farmer, sailor, trader and explorer as he did fighting; and he had to provide his own equipment.

Armor to protect the body took many hours of skilled work to make. It was certainly expensive, and was probably worn only by Viking leaders and their picked household warriors. The other fighting men would have worn their everyday clothes, relying on an iron helmet and a sturdy wooden shield for protection.

The sword was the most admired and honored weapon, and many Vikings would have carried one. The other weapon, which became almost the trademark of the Norsemen, was the heavy, two-handed battleaxe. This fearsome weapon, swung by a big, muscular man, could shear through any armor. Some warriors are said to have been able to behead a horse at a blow. Men who could afford neither sword nor axe used a thrusting spear.

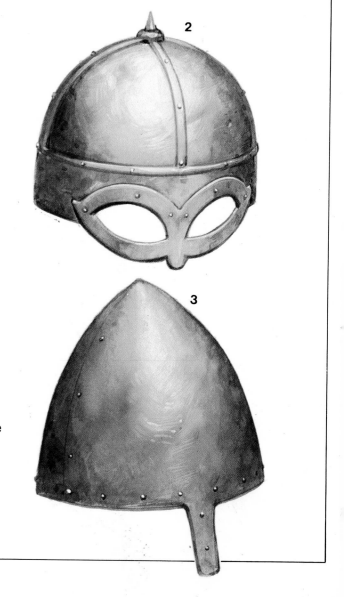

△**1** Swedish iron and bronze helmet of the 7th century, about 150 years before the Viking age of c. 790–1060.
2 Clearly descended from the 7th-century helmet is this simpler type, worn by many Vikings of the 800s and 900s. The horned and winged helmets seen in Hollywood films are pure fiction!
3 Usually called a Norman helmet, this type of iron cap with a nose-bar to guard the face was also widely used by Viking warriors.

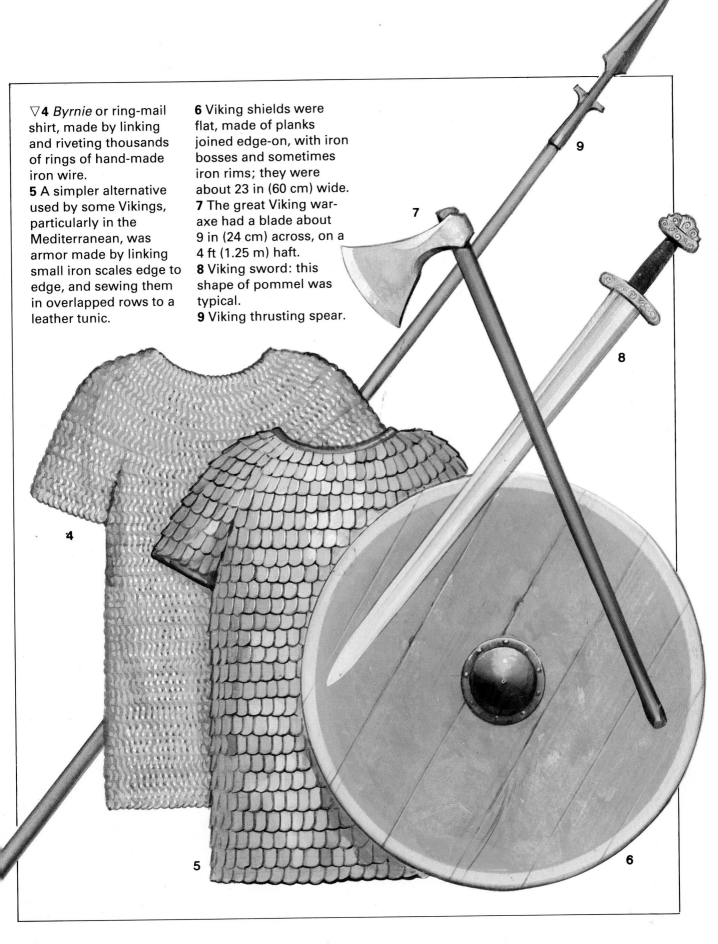

▽**4** *Byrnie* or ring-mail shirt, made by linking and riveting thousands of rings of hand-made iron wire.

5 A simpler alternative used by some Vikings, particularly in the Mediterranean, was armor made by linking small iron scales edge to edge, and sewing them in overlapped rows to a leather tunic.

6 Viking shields were flat, made of planks joined edge-on, with iron bosses and sometimes iron rims; they were about 23 in (60 cm) wide.

7 The great Viking war-axe had a blade about 9 in (24 cm) across, on a 4 ft (1.25 m) haft.

8 Viking sword: this shape of pommel was typical.

9 Viking thrusting spear.

The magic in the steel

Warlike peoples have always admired fine weapons and armor. The Vikings were an artistic people and decorated their best weapons with the entwined patterns which they loved. They held the sword in particularly high regard.

In the sagas recited by the Viking *skalds*, or minstrels, the sword was called the "gray battle-ice." A fine blade was valued not only for its balance and temper, but even for having a particular personality. Individual swords were given names, such as "Skull-biter" or "Foe's bane." The name was sometimes engraved on the blade in runes, a type of sign-writing used by the Norsemen. Special marks of respected smiths or words of good omen might also be included. The hilts were often expensively decorated with silver, gold, copper, and colored enamel-work of great beauty.

Some weapons were buried with their owners when they died. Others were handed down from generation to generation. They were believed to pass on some of the skill and luck of the warriors who had wielded them – Vikings respected luck above all else. Spears and axes covered with patterns of inlaid silver wire have also been found, so they, too, must have been cherished by the Viking warriors.

▽ A Viking smith hammers out the shape of a blade. The iron has been heated red-hot in a charcoal furnace fed by bellows. Frequent heating and quenching in cold water hardened the metal. The superstitious Vikings believed that a certain amount of magic, as well as skilled craftsmanship, went into the best weapons.

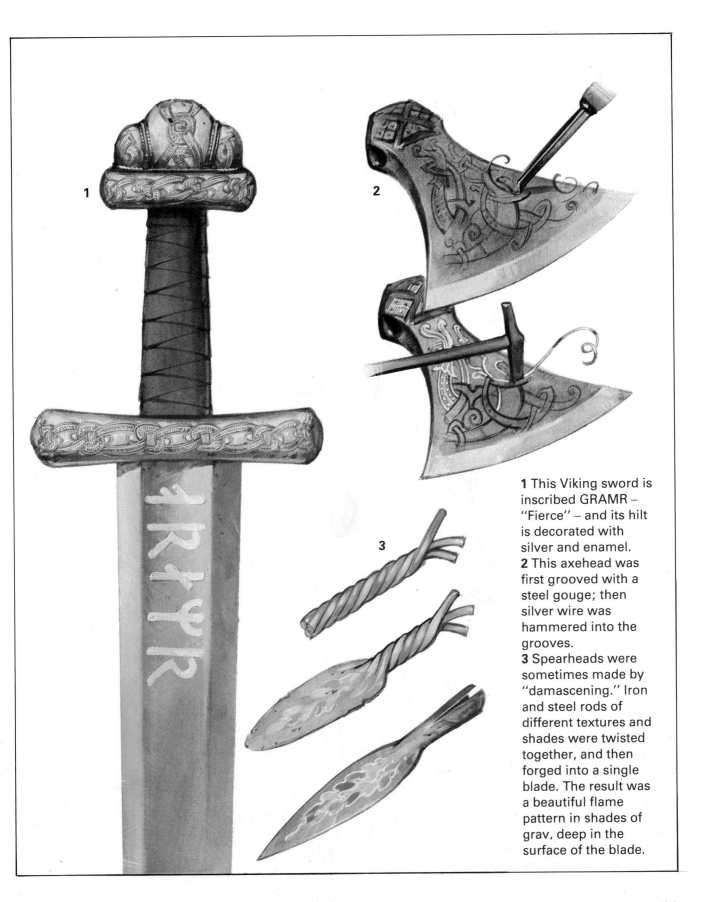

1 This Viking sword is inscribed GRAMR – "Fierce" – and its hilt is decorated with silver and enamel.

2 This axehead was first grooved with a steel gouge; then silver wire was hammered into the grooves.

3 Spearheads were sometimes made by "damascening." Iron and steel rods of different textures and shades were twisted together, and then forged into a single blade. The result was a beautiful flame pattern in shades of grav, deep in the surface of the blade.

Mobility and stealth

Because of their shallow draft, Viking dragon ships could sail far up rivers, or beach at high-tide mark on gently shelving coasts. Other ships of the period needed deeper water, and so were limited to proper ports. This gave Viking raiders the advantage of surprise: they could land without warning at almost any point along the shoreline.

Raiding ships would slip up a river estuary under cover of night or foggy weather. Raids usually lasted several days.

The ships would be beached, and a defended base camp set up. Favorite spots were low islands or sand spits, surrounded by creeks and mud flats. This made it difficult for local warriors to attack Viking camps either on foot or by boat.

Fanning out from their base to scour the countryside, the Vikings often captured horses to give them greater range and speed. They were used only for transport, however; the Viking was no cavalryman,

▷Guiding their ship carefully through the shallows, a Viking crew steals ashore. Longships could be rowed anywhere the water was waist-deep. In the 8th and 9th centuries Europe was thinly populated, so it was easy for the raiders to approach their victims unseen, and to keep their base camp hidden for a few days.

and fought on foot. Frequent targets for raids were isolated towns or farming villages, as well as monasteries. Church property was poorly defended and offered rich plunder. Monasteries and abbeys often had precious silver objects; and in those days, too, people living nearby sometimes lodged their valuables with the priests for safe-keeping, like a modern bank.

Large-scale attacks sometimes involved a great fleet of ships, but they used much the same tactics as single raiding crews. In the late 800s Viking fleets sailed far up the great rivers of France and pillaged cities on their banks. Paris was attacked three times; Lyons, Orleans, Rouen and Amiens all felt the "fury of the Norsemen." As late as 1010, Olaf Haraldsson of Norway sailed up the Thames and destroyed London Bridge; he covered his ships with brushwood roofs to protect them from the arrows and spears of the Saxons on the banks.

The fury of the Northmen

The horror of Viking raids terrified the almost helpless peoples of western Europe. They had no permanent armies to protect them; and since news traveled no faster than a galloping horse, it took far too long to raise the alarm and gather enough fighting men to catch the raiders before they reached their ships again. Usually, rescue parties found only burned-out buildings and unburied dead. The Vikings cut down defenseless peasants and priests without mercy; the only men who might be spared were dragged off, with the women, to be sold into slavery. No wonder the Christians of the ninth century prayed: "From the fury of the Northmen, deliver us, O Lord!"

▽ A Viking war band ravages a monastery and its village. Cattle are run off, anything of value is seized, and the rest is set on fire. Christian priests were thought to be unlucky at sea. Any who might be spared and taken prisoner were thrown overboard at the first hint of bad weather during the raiders' voyage home.

Feasting a victory

Vikings went on their expeditions between the spring sowing and the autumn harvest. Summer was the best sailing weather; and the womenfolk and slaves could manage the farms on their own.

Viking women were strong and independent. They sometimes fought beside their men to defend their homes; and their legal rights were greater than those of "civilized" women many centuries later. They were expert weavers of fine cloth. Men and women alike had rich clothes and jewelry for special occasions such as a feast to celebrate a homecoming.

Despite their prowess as sailors and fighters, Vikings often died at sea or in battle; the real risks made their homecoming, laden with booty, doubly exciting. Great feasts would be held in the halls shared by large families and their followers. The chief would reward his best warriors with gifts; captured weapons were prized, as were heavy gold rings to wear on the arms or to attach to sword hilts. Generosity was expected of a leader, if he was to keep his followers.

▷Vikings loved feasts, with huge meals, ale-drinking, and singing. They ate meat, game, fish, peas, beans, leeks, apples, nuts and berries. Minstrels recited heroic story-poems to harp-music. Smoke from fires built on central hearths escaped through holes in the roof. Wide platforms on each side of the hall were used as communal beds, though important family members had cupboard beds in the walls.

"The whale's road"

The finest seamen of their age, the Norsemen were the first to sail regularly far out of sight of land. We do not know how they found their way in strange waters. They used the sun and stars as guides; but, despite tales of a "sun-stone," they are not believed to have had compasses.

Their ships were strong and cleverly built to withstand heavy weather. But it was still horribly dangerous to sail into the unknown North Atlantic in an open boat only about as long as five automobiles! Many ships must have vanished without trace, but adventurers still pushed off each spring on "the whale's road" – their name for the open oceans.

When they followed coastlines closely, they built up a store of knowledge to help them find their way. They noted everything – the flight of seabirds, the shoaling of fish, the types of weed and sand they passed, the exact speed and direction of wind and current, the landmarks on shore, the very taste of the salt water in different places.

▷Viking sailors fight to ride out a sudden Atlantic squall. Incredibly brave and hardy, they sailed into unknown waters with little idea of when or where they would find land. They lived on open decks, eating cold food and sleeping in two-man leather sleeping-bags for a little warmth. Storms and fighting often cost Viking expeditions as many as a third or half of their ships and men.

Danes and Norwegians mostly sailed south and west, down both sides of Britain. They settled on the Faeroe, Shetland, Orkney and Hebridean islands; in Ireland, England and Normandy; and in Iceland. The Norwegian Eric the Red led settlers from Iceland to Greenland in the 980s. His son Leif landed in Newfoundland in about 1000, but attempts to settle permanently in America – "Vinland" – were to fail.

Sailing the Mediterranean, Vikings raided the coasts of Spain, southern France, Italy and North Africa. Swedish Vikings crossed the Baltic eastwards, and sailed up the rivers deep into Russia, even reaching Persia across the Caspian Sea.

▽ The main Viking routes. They crossed Russia by manhandling ships overland from river to river. The Dnieper led them south to the Black Sea; the Volga east to the Caspian.

Miklagard the Golden

The greatest city of the ninth-century world was Constantinople – known today as Istanbul. The Vikings called it Miklagard, the "Great City." It was the capital of the Byzantine Empire, ruling what had been the eastern half of the old Roman Empire. Rich, powerful and sophisticated, this city of gold and marble had a million inhabitants, at a time when Western capitals were rough townships of a few thousand. It was not long before the wealth of the "Greeks" (as Westerners called the Byzantines) caught the interest of the Norsemen.

Sailing down the Dnieper River, ambassadors from the Rus – the Swedish colonies in central Russia – reached the city by about 838 AD. Twenty years later some 200 Viking longships followed and tried to sack Constantinople. They failed: the huge walls and sophisticated army that confronted them were a far cry from the stockades and war bands of the West.

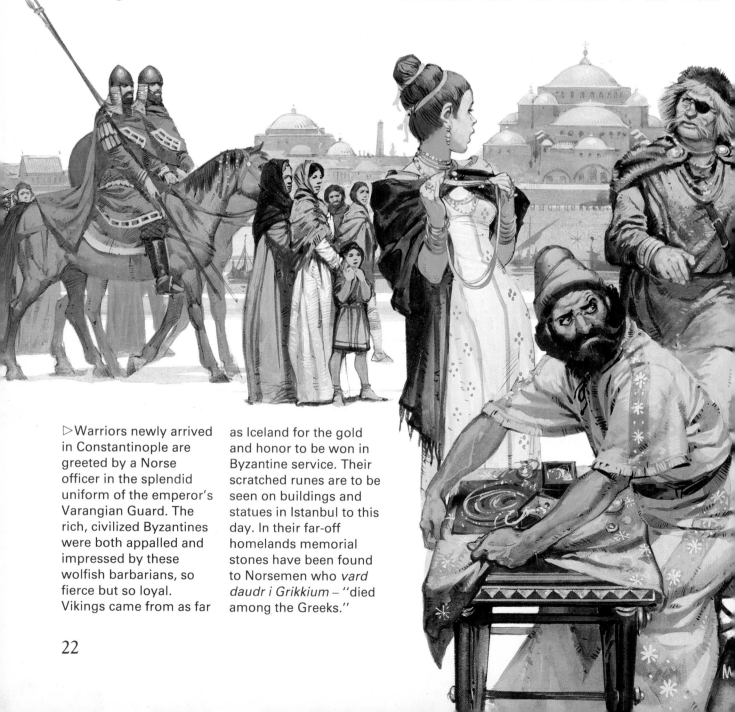

▷Warriors newly arrived in Constantinople are greeted by a Norse officer in the splendid uniform of the emperor's Varangian Guard. The rich, civilized Byzantines were both appalled and impressed by these wolfish barbarians, so fierce but so loyal. Vikings came from as far as Iceland for the gold and honor to be won in Byzantine service. Their scratched runes are to be seen on buildings and statues in Istanbul to this day. In their far-off homelands memorial stones have been found to Norsemen who *vard daudr i Grikkium* – "died among the Greeks."

Even so, their attacks so impressed the Byzantines that they agreed to a treaty.

The Byzantines also allowed Vikings to enlist in the mercenary Varangian Guard. These axemen won great renown in Byzantine campaigns all over the eastern Mediterranean world, and as loyal bodyguards. Among many Norse heroes to serve in the Guard was Harald Hardraada, later king of Norway, who commanded the Varangians in about AD 1033–45.

Traders from the world's end

During what used to be called the Dark Ages, from the fifth to the eleventh century, the Old World was actually covered by a web of busy trade routes. Goods and travelers journeyed between Europe, Africa, the Middle East, Asia, India and China. Scandinavia was the northern end of this system, and goods from all over the world have been found there.

The Vikings sent their own traders out in all directions. In the ninth century Swedish crews sailed up the rivers into the heart of Russia. By AD 860 they actually ruled the local Slavs from the towns of Kiev and Novgorod. Russia is named after these Norsemen, who were called "the Rus." Here, as in other countries, the Norse conquerors eventually intermarried and faded into the local population; but in Russia their rule lasted at least until AD 1020.

For some 200 years each summer brought traders from all over the world up Russia's rivers to Norse trading posts. They took some risk of being ambushed by their more ruthless customers.

At trading posts in Russia the Vikings met

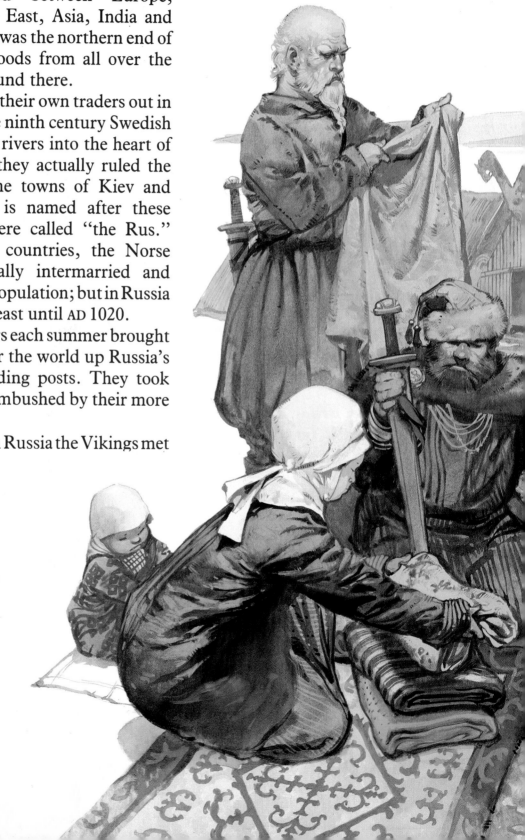

▷A Norse trading post on the Volga River. Permanent cabins were built here, but tents were also put up for seasonal visitors. Vikings brought honey, amber, swords, furs, cloth, leather and above all the slaves they captured in their raids. They traded them for silver, glassware, wine, spices and even silks from far-off China.

24

Arab travelers, who wrote eye-witness descriptions. Arab ambassadors and scholars, such as Ibn Fadlan, were among the most sophisticated people of that time. They were impressed by the Norsemen, "tall as date palms, blond and ruddy;" but shocked by their ignorance, drunken violence, horrible singing and lack of cleanliness! Ibn Fadlan called them "the filthiest of God's creatures." But what must English Anglo-Saxons have been like – they complained that Vikings were *too* clean! The English thought that combing the hair, and bathing and even changing clothes each week, were slick foreign tricks designed to sweep Saxon ladies off their feet!

Viking armies

In some places Norse raids were frequent enough to completely ruin or drive away the local people. Here the Vikings began to stay all year round, making winter camps between summer campaigns. Later they sent for their families. By the late ninth century there were large, permanent settlements, and "armies" of several hundred Vikings fought frontier wars against their neighbors. This was, in fact, a weakness.

The Norse settlers had lost the advantage of surprise. Now *they* had nearby homes which had to be defended and it was possible for enemies to plan wars against them, knowing roughly where they were. The Franks of northern France, and the Saxons of Wessex in southern England, slowly and painfully learned how to assemble large armies against the Vikings. In the end the Vikings, never very numerous, were beaten. They were confined to their own regions as peaceful neighbors.

In pitched battles Vikings fought without complicated tactics, just like other warriors of their time. They simply formed a tight mass around their chiefs, making a "shield-wall." They hacked at the enemy hand-to-hand until one side lost so many men that they had to run. The strength and bravery of the individual man, and loyalty to his chief, were all that mattered. The Viking religion glorified war and death in battle. If a chief fell, his bodyguard of picked warriors, whom he had supported and rewarded during his life, were expected to die around his body.

◁Surrounded by Frankish warriors, Vikings sell their lives dearly around their raven banner. The carrion-bird of the battlefield, the raven was a typically grim Viking symbol of death. The Franks also raised troops of horse-men, whose better mobility helped them cut off and trap Viking bands.

Through the flames to Valhalla

The fierce religion of the Vikings taught that only those who died in battle enjoyed the full rewards of the afterlife. Warriors actually feared a shameful "straw-death" faced peacefully in bed.

When a warrior died, his body was burned on a funeral pyre. After lying in state for some days, the corpse was arrayed in rich clothing and laid on a bed in a ship, under a canopy of expensive material. Vikings believed that anything burned with the dead man accompanied him into the afterlife. His property was divided into three: a third for his family, a third for funeral goods, and a third to pay for drink at the funeral feast.

The dead man's weapons and war gear were laid close at hand, and food and drink were also placed within reach. Some of his horses and cattle were slaughtered and added to the pyre. A slave girl might volunteer for the honor of going with her master to serve him beyond the grave. She would be drugged, then quickly killed and laid beside him. Finally, the ship and all it contained were burned to ashes.

▷A Viking funeral, as witnessed on the banks of the Volga in Russia in the year 922 by the Arab traveler Ibn Fadlan. An old crone, called "the angel of death," presided over the grisly rites, and killed the slave girl who volunteered to die alongside her master. The dead man's nearest male relative, ritually naked, threw the first blazing torch; then everyone present added a burning branch.

The Vikings believed that when a man died in battle, the great god Odin sent heavenly warrior-maidens called Valkyries riding across the sky to gather up his soul and carry it to Valhalla. In this heavenly hall he would spend eternity, fighting all day and feasting all night. At the end of time his soul would fight beside the gods in a last, doomed battle against evil.

◁ A Viking image of Thor, the god of the skies and the storm, holding his hammer symbol.

Glossary

Amber Fossilized resin found on the shore – a precious substance used for jewelry and small decorative objects.

Byrnie Norse name for a shirt of iron ring-mail armor.

Byzantine Empire Great power based on the city of Constantinople: the former eastern half of the Roman Empire.

Draft The depth of water needed to float a particular ship.

Franks The Germanic peoples who occupied France, the Low Countries and West Germany after the fall of the Roman Empire in the west in the fifth century.

Gunwale The top edge of a ship's side.

Hall Large house, usually made of timber. Viking families of many relatives, and their servants, lived in single halls.

Keel The deep timber beam forming the central "spine" of the bottom of a ship.

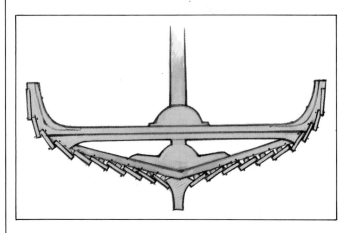

Knot Measurement of speed at sea: 6,080 ft (one nautical mile) per hour.

Navigation The science of finding out a ship's position at sea, and finding the way to a particular destination.

Pagan A person who followed a religion other than Christianity, Judaism or Islam.

Pommel The end of a sword-hilt, often finished off with a decorated knob.

Rivet A metal peg or nail, hammered into two pieces of wood or metal to hold them together.

Rudder Steering device for a ship: a flat oar or board fixed at the stern, edge-on to the water.

Runes Type of sign-writing used by the people of Scandinavia from about AD 200. A short alphabet was made up of different patterns of criss-crossing straight lines.

Saga Long poem telling the story of the deeds of Norse adventurers.

Saxons Germanic peoples who emigrated from north Germany in the fifth and sixth centuries, invading and settling in England.

Skald A Norse minstrel who made up and memorized sagas, reciting them at feasts, sometimes to harp accompaniment. More than just entertainers, they were the men who recorded Viking history for later generations.

Stem The central wooden beam at the bow of a ship – the front end of the keel. Vikings often carved the top of the stem-post into a fantastic beast-head, so the ships were called "dragon-ships."

Temper The degree of hardness in a piece of worked metal, particularly a weapon blade.

Tiller The lever by which a ship's helmsman controls the angle of the rudder to steer the ship.

Yardarm The long cross-piece or spar on the mast of a ship, to which the sail is attached.

Timechart

789 Three Norse ships land in Dorset, southern England; local Saxons killed.

793 First Viking raid on Lindisfarne, an island monastery off northeast England, marks the start of the so-called Viking age.

830s Raids on England and France become more frequent, stronger, and co-ordinated. Norwegians invade Ireland.

850–51 Danish Vikings winter in England for the first time, a sign of permanent settlement to come. London and Canterbury are sacked, but the Danes are later beaten at Ockley, Surrey.

850s–860s Huge, repeated raids up the rivers of France lay waste large areas. A fleet sails from the Loire estuary to the Mediterranean, raiding along the coasts of Spain, southern France, Italy and North Africa. First attacks on Constantinople.

870s See-saw series of campaigns between the advancing Norsemen, and the Saxon defenders of the last free kingdom in England – Wessex, in the southwest. After many setbacks Alfred the Great of Wessex finally defeats the Norse. They agree to stay in their own territories (the Danelaw) and their king accepts Christianity.

885 The Île de la Cité in the Seine holds out during a year-long Viking siege of Paris.

890s The Viking "Great Army" crosses from France to England, threatening Wessex once more. In a four-year campaign Alfred builds the first English warships, founds a chain of defensive forts, and organizes a local militia. Defeated, the Great Army departs.

911 Repeated attacks on Constantinople finally win the Rus, under Oleg of Kiev and Novgorod, trading rights in the city and recruitment in the Byzantine army.

913 King Charles the Simple of France gives the Viking leader Hrolf the Ganger legal title to lands in northern France, which he has already pillaged: this becomes the Duchy of Normandy.

937 At the end of long years of effort by Alfred's son Edward and grandson Athelstan, a last great Viking rising is put down. Wessex is recognized as the greatest power in England; and in **959** the country is finally unified under King Edgar of Wessex.

968 The Irish king Brian Boru sacks the Norse town of Limerick during his lifelong fight against the Irish Vikings.

983 Eric the Red explores and later colonizes Greenland.

991–1012 Repeated payment of Danegeld (bribes) to buy off a new wave of threatening Vikings finally costs weak King Ethelred of Wessex his throne. Norse power increases again.

c.1000 Leif Ericsson explores Vinland (Newfoundland coast). Later colonists fail after three years in North America.

1014 The aged Brian Boru is killed at the moment of victory over Irish Vikings at battle of Clontarf.

1016–27 Most Norsemen now accept Christianity. Knut of Norway briefly makes himself King of England, Norway and Denmark.

1066 Harald Hardraada of Norway killed in battle of Stamford Bridge, near York, by Harold Godwinsson's Saxons. Normans invade England under William the Conqueror. The close of the Viking age.

Index

PRINTED IN BELGIUM BY
proost
INTERNATIONAL BOOK PRODUCTION

REFERENCE

REFERENCE